Clifton Church

Dallas, Texas, through a Camera

Clifton Church

Dallas, Texas, through a Camera

ISBN/EAN: 9783744756952

Printed in Europe, USA, Canada, Australia, Japan

Cover: Foto ©Thomas Meinert / pixelio.de

More available books at **www.hansebooks.com**

DALLAS
TEXAS

Through a Camera

. . .

A Collection of Half=Tone Engravings

from Original Photographs by

———— Clifton Church.

. . . . . .

DALLAS, TEXAS:
J. W. COLVILLE, FRANKLIN PRINTING HOUSE,
1894.

DALLAS COUNTY COURT HOUSE.

VIEW ON MAIN STREET.

CITY HALL.

VIEW ON ELM STREET.

POST OFFICE. U. S. GOVERNMENT BUILDING.

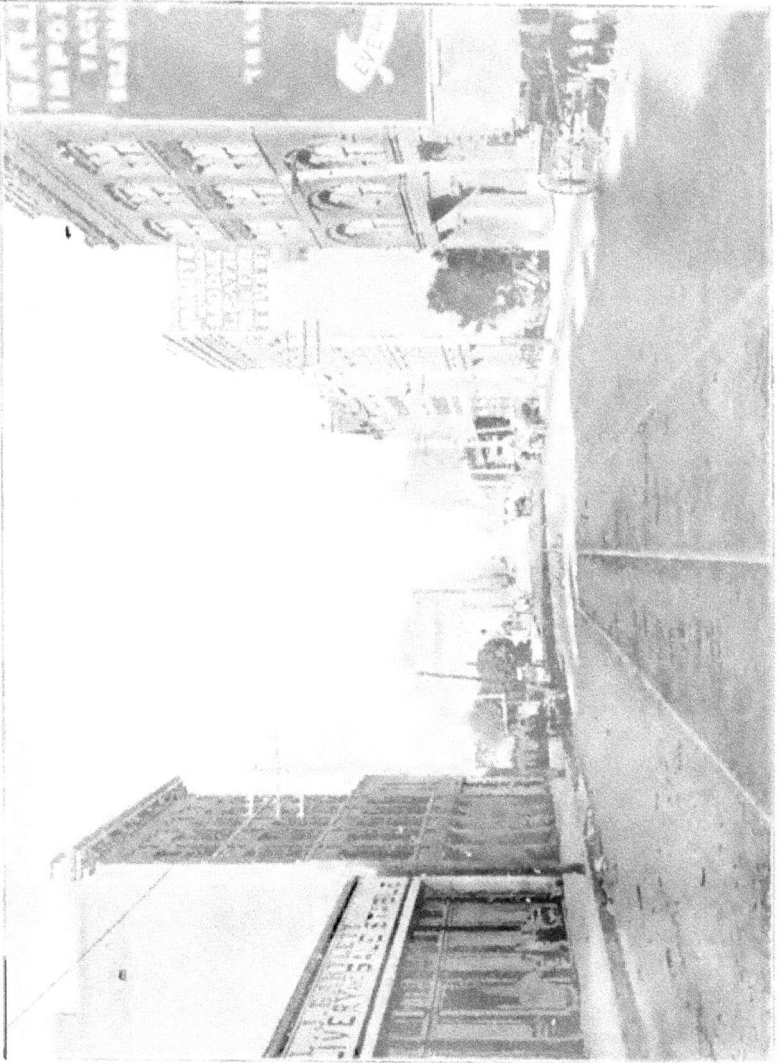

BALLARD, WEBB & BURNETTE CO. BUILDING.

ORIENTAL HOTEL. W J ALDEN, MANAGER.

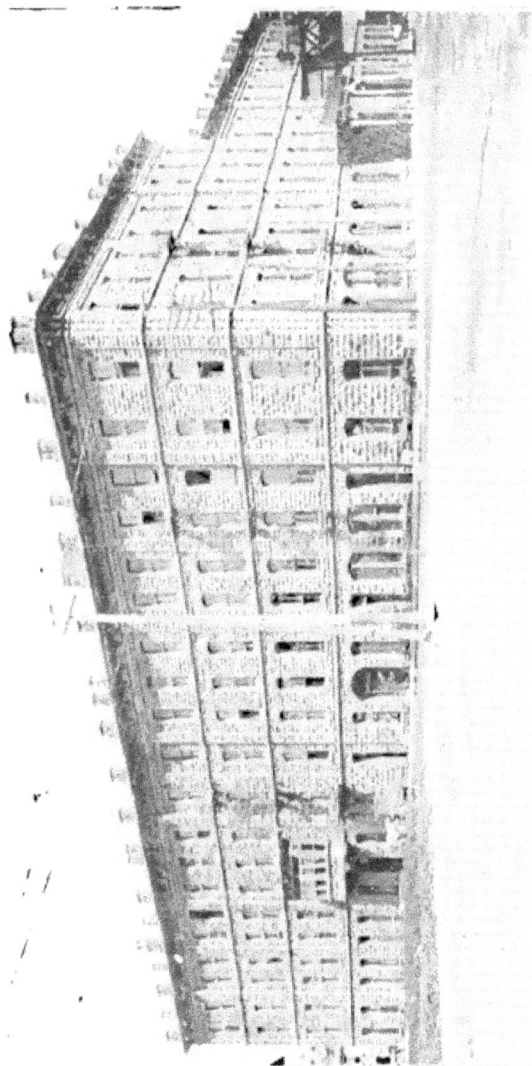

NORTH TEXAS BUILDING.

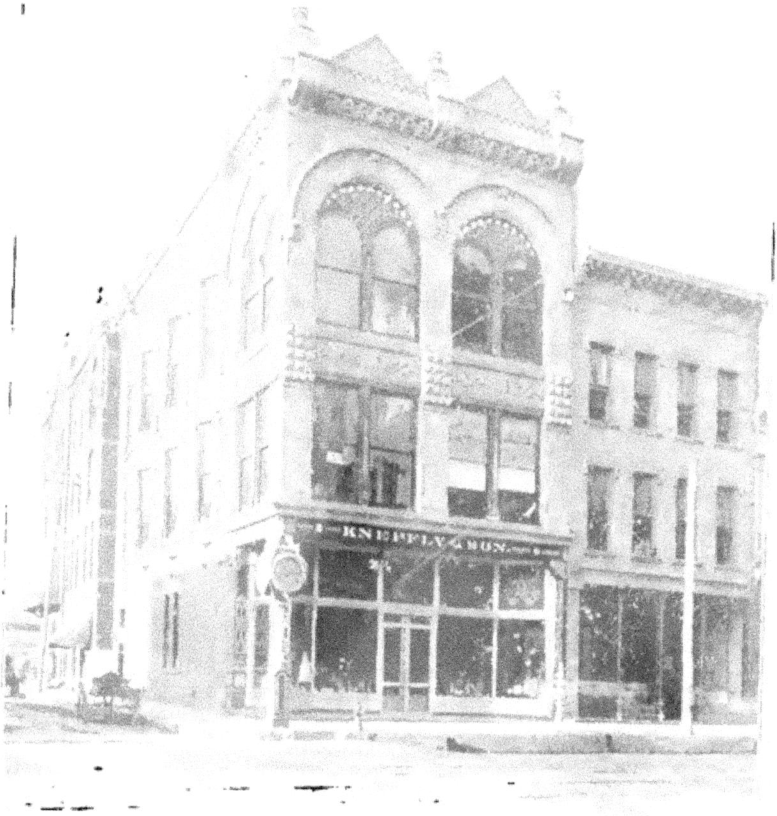
KNEPFLY & SON.

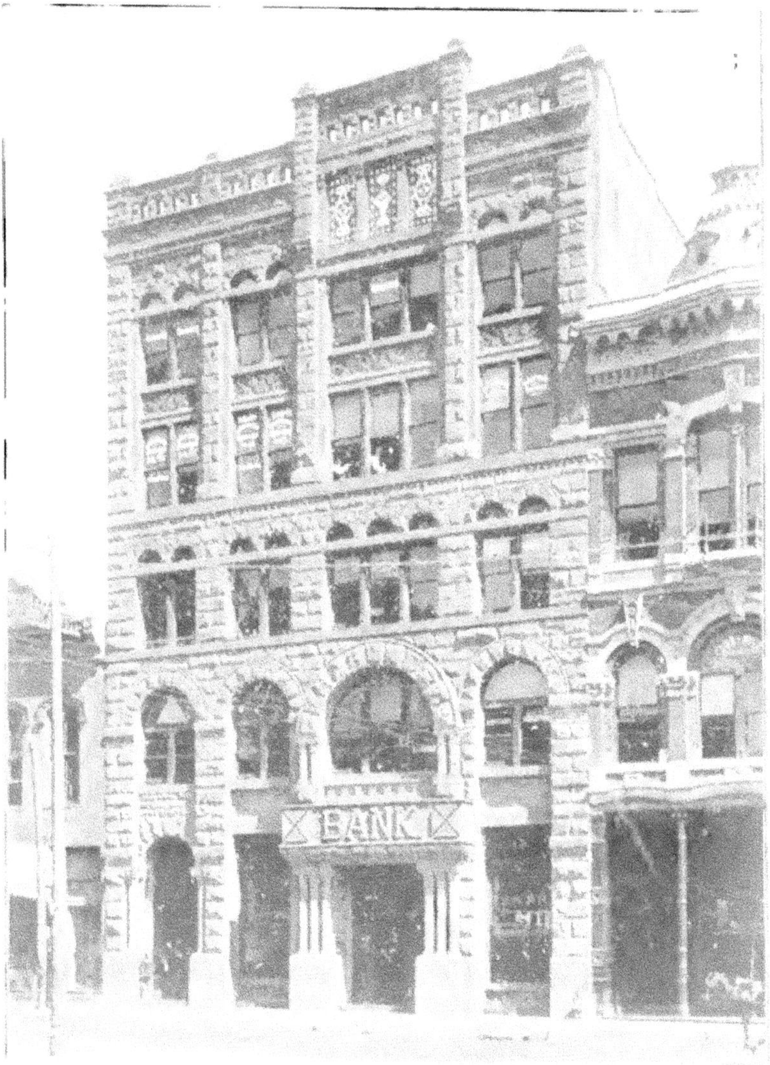
BANK

GOULD BUILDING. GENERAL OFFICES T. & P. R. R.

MIDDLETON BUILDING

SCOLLARD BUILDINGS.

DALLAS CLUB

DALLAS OPERA HOUSE

THE MK AND T

Missouri Kansas & Texas Railway

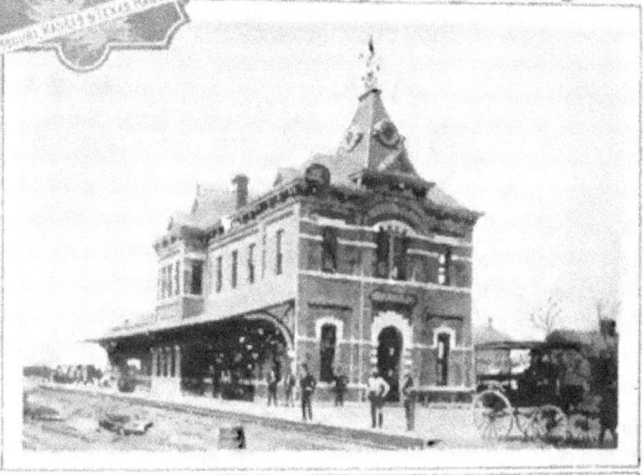

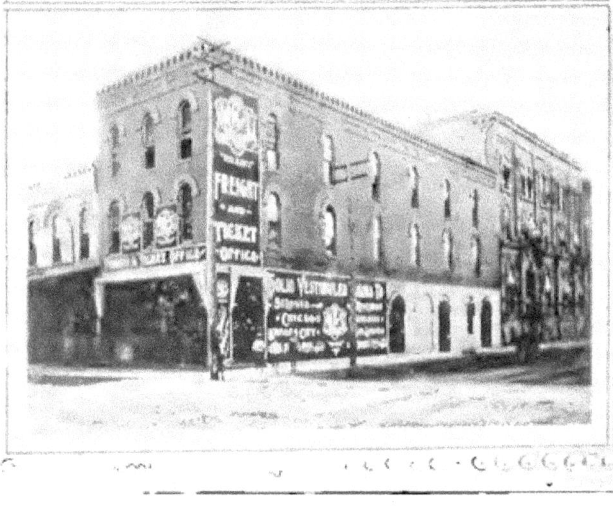

CHURCHES.

RESIDENCES.

RESIDENCES.

MANUFACTORIES.

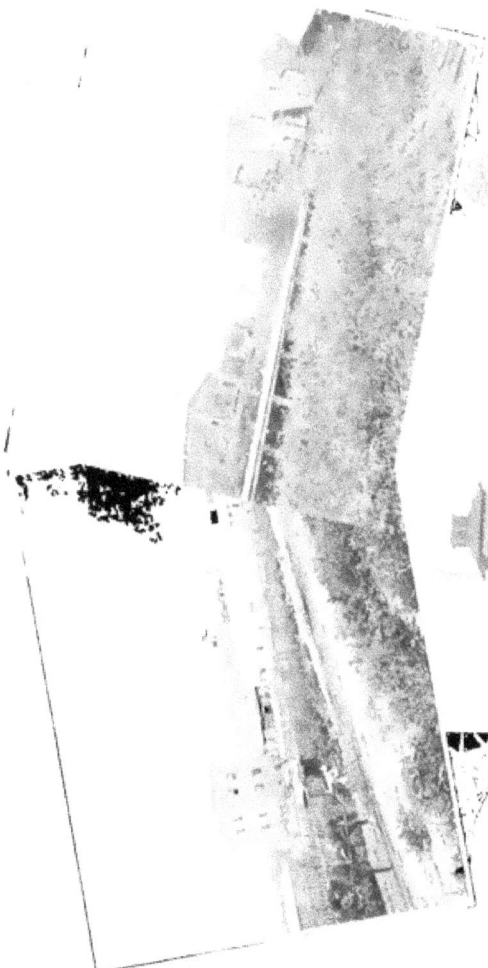

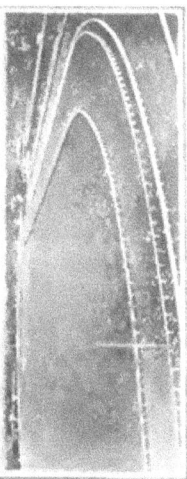

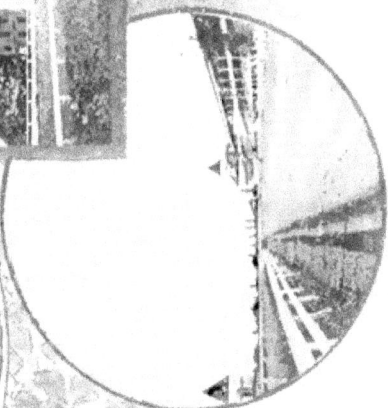

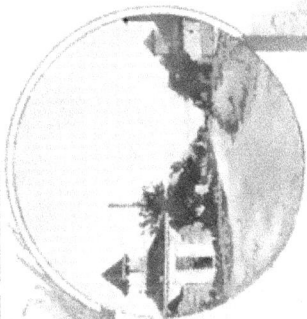

OAK CLIFF.

CENTRAL SCHOOL.
OAK CLIFF FEMALE COLLEGE.

PAVILION.
ARMORY. D. L. A.

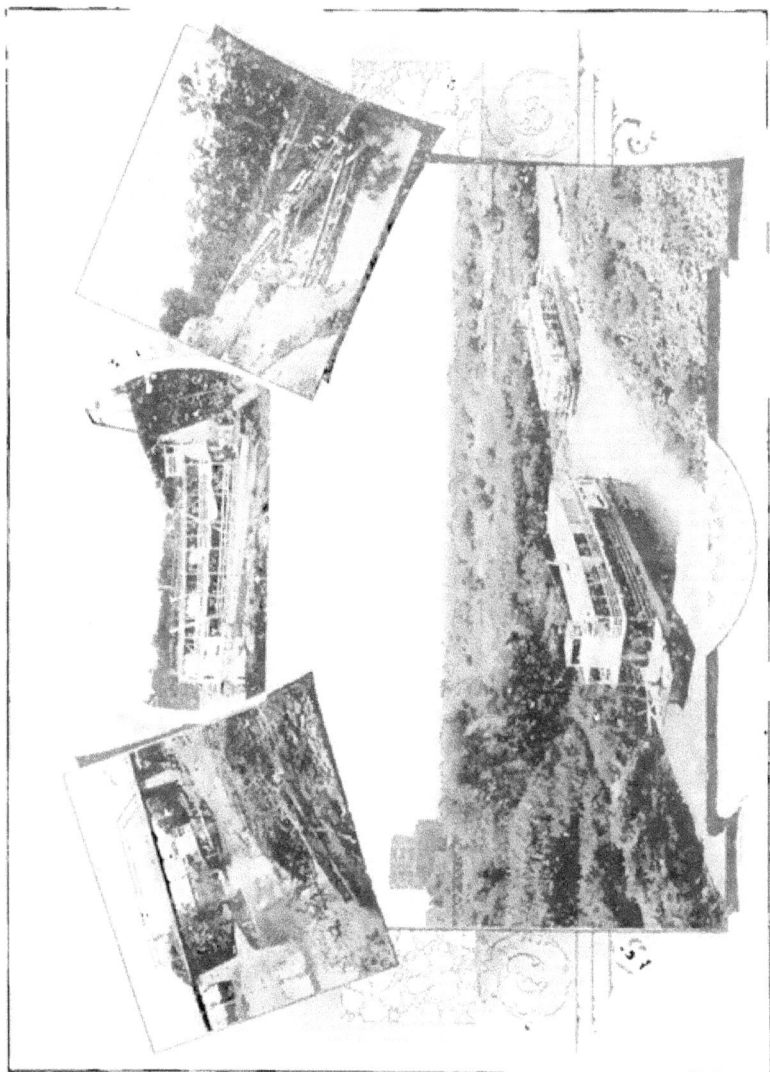

www.ingramcontent.com/pod-product-compliance
Lightning Source LLC
Chambersburg PA
CBHW022146090426
42742CB00010B/1413